SEEKING FORTUNE

DURING THE CALIFORNIA GOLD RUSH

A HISTORY SEEKING ADVENTURE

by Matt Doeden

CAPSTONE PRESS
a capstone imprint

Published by You Choose, an imprint of Capstone
1710 Roe Crest Drive, North Mankato, Minnesota 56003
capstonepub.com

Library of Congress Cataloging-in-Publication Data is available on the Library of
Congress website.

ISBN: 9781669032540 (hardcover)
ISBN: 9781669032731 (paperback)
ISBN: 9781669032649 (ebook PDF)

Summary: YOU are one of the many fortune seekers during the California Gold
Rush in the 1850s. Will you pan for gold, set up a mine, or make your riches by
serving the miners who have flocked to the area? Step back in time to face the
challenges and decisions that real people faced during this exciting time in history.

Editorial Credits
Editor: Mandy Robbins; Designer: Heidi Thompson; Media Researcher: Jo Miller;
Production Specialist: Tori Abraham

Image Credits
Alamy: INTERFOTO, 79, Pictures Now, 70, The History Collection, 9; Getty
Images: bauhaus1000, 4, benoitb, Cover, Bettmann, 30, Cannasue, 94, Hulton
Archive, 46, ilbusca, 55, mikroman6, 90, powerofforever, 35, 61, RockingStock,
77, Stock Montage, 50; Library of Congress, 18, 33, 85, 103, 107; Shutterstock:
Atmosphere1, 105, Everett Collection, 25, kenkistler, 15, Tom Reichner, 39

All internet sites appearing in back matter were available and accurate when this
book was sent to press.

TABLE OF CONTENTS

ABOUT YOUR ADVENTURE

YOU are living in California at the height of the Gold Rush. This exciting time period lasted from 1848 through the 1850s. The discovery of gold has sent shock waves through the nation.

People are flocking west by the thousands. Fortunes are being built . . . and lives are being lost. Do you have the skill—and the luck—to strike it rich in the rugged California wilderness? YOU CHOOSE which paths to take. Will you risk it all or play it safe? Will you thrive or fall to ruin?

Turn the page to begin your adventure.

CHAPTER 1

GOLD!

"Gold!" shouts a voice. A young man runs through the streets of a dusty California town. He waves his arms in the air. "I found it! Gold!"

You can't help but smile. It feels like the whole world has gold fever. Ever since the precious metal was discovered at Sutter's Mill in 1848, the California Gold Rush has been on. People from around the country—and the world—are flocking to the hills of northern California to seek their fortunes.

Turn the page.

You don't blame the man for his excitement. Like so many others, you are hoping to strike it rich. But the truth is, it's not that easy. For every prospector who lives the dream, there are many more who fail. Some even lose their lives in the process. Gold is big business. Everyone wants their piece of the rush. Some people are willing to lie, steal, cheat, and even kill to get it.

You'll have to use your wits if you want to strike it rich. It will take smarts, hard work, and a whole lot of luck to be one of the few who succeed.

There are many paths to success. Many prospectors turn to panning. It's as simple as it sounds—using a metal pan to search for nuggets of gold in streams and rivers. Some get more serious, digging into rocky land in search of big strikes. Others don't look for gold at all. They seek out opportunities running shops, banks, and other business that prospectors need.

Any path can lead to riches—or disaster.

It's all about the choices you make.

- To try your luck at panning, turn to page 11.
- To get your pickaxe and start digging, turn to page 45.
- To work in a booming Gold Rush town, turn to page 75.

CHAPTER 2

A FLASH IN THE PAN

The sun beats down on you. Sweat drips into your eyes. Carefully, you make your way down a rocky ravine. Each step is an adventure, as rock crumbles away beneath your feet.

As much as you're struggling to find safe footing, the young woman in front of you seems completely at home. Her steps are effortless, barely shifting the rocks below at all. Kalapine looks back over her shoulder. Her long, dark hair blows in the wind. "Almost there," she says. Her English is good, but she says little.

Turn the page.

Like you, Kalapine is still a teenager. But she knows the land well. She's a member of the Miwok people, who have lived here in the lower parts of the Sierra Madre mountain region all her life. The Gold Rush has had a big impact on the Miwok, as well as other native peoples in this part of California. Prospectors have swarmed over their homelands, often driving the Miwok away. Kalapine is making the best of a bad situation, leading prospectors out to rivers, streams, and mining sites deep in the wilderness for a fee. She's your guide, and you can't imagine making your way out here without her.

It's been a long day of hiking already. As afternoon temperatures soar, the gear-loaded pack on your back feels heavier by the moment. But just when you think you can't go any farther, Kalapine stops. She points down into the ravine, where a small river—a tributary of the Kern River—winds through trees and rocks.

"This is one place," she says. As you gaze down onto the river, you see several camps set up along its banks. A few people are standing in the water, stooped over metal pans.

"Is this the best place?" you ask.

Kalapine shrugs. "It is an easy place. Close to towns. Close to supplies."

You nod. Those are good features. But it's clear that quite a few others have the same thought. Does that mean it's a good site for panning gold? Or are people just here because it's close?

"How far is it to something less . . . popular?" you ask.

Kalapine gazes off into the distance. "If you want a stream for yourself, it's another half a day. But it's much more dangerous to be alone in the deep wilderness. You should stay here."

Turn the page.

You groan. The thought of hiking another half day is not appealing. And knowing that you'll be that much farther from civilization is a concern. Is it worth the extra work and risk to reach a site that's less populated? Or is it possible that the crowd of people down by this river is a sign that gold is plentiful here?

Kalapine looks at you, awaiting your reply.

- To try this site, turn to page 16.
- To continue deeper into the wilderness, turn to page 25.

It's probably safer to be closer to civilization. You slowly nod your head as you look down at the river below. "This will do. Thank you."

Kalapine smiles. "Good luck," she tells you.

The two of you part ways. You make your way down to the riverbank, where several small campsites stand.

"Hello there!" calls out an older man. He's sitting over a small fire, cooking a piece of fish in a cast-iron pan. It smells good, and your stomach rumbles.

You wave back. The man stands up to greet you. He sticks out his hand and introduces himself.

"I'm Abraham. Welcome to the river. I've got a big walleye cooking. You're welcome to join me if you're hungry."

You hesitate. In your short time in California, you've come to believe that nobody offers you something for nothing. And you really want to get yourself set up and start panning for gold. Your head tells you to decline the invitation. But your stomach wants you to accept.

- To join Abraham, turn to page 18.
- To decline, turn to page 21.

357. "We have it Rich." - Washing and
panning gold. Rockerville, Dak.

Men panning for gold

You're eager to get started. But it's been a long
journey, and the chance to sit down and eat is too
good to pass up. You spend the next hour with
Abraham. He's kind and tells you everything
he knows about the stream. You learn where to
look, where the current is dangerous, and which
prospectors to avoid.

"There's gold in this stream," he assures you. "I've been out here a month. So far, I haven't had much luck, but others have. My lucky strike is coming. I can feel it."

"Thanks for the fish and the company," you tell Abraham. "I think it's time I start panning."

Abraham pats you on the shoulder and wishes you luck.

One good thing about panning for gold is that the equipment is simple and easy to use. You bring your metal pan down to the river's edge, scoop up some gravel and water, and start to swirl it. As you gently swirl, the water and lighter gravel spill over the edges. Soon, you're left with just the heavier material. You sift through it, searching for the telltale glimmer of gold.

Turn the page.

Nothing. You shrug. Panning takes time. You could hardly expect to get it on your first try.

You move down the riverbank, until you find a spot that looks promising. Along a bend, a bank of fine sand lies below a swift current. Again, you load up your pan and swirl. After 28 tries, something glints brightly in the sun.

Your breath catches in your throat. Carefully, you pull out a small, brilliant pebble. A quick test with your teeth confirms the find. It's soft metal. It's a tiny gold nugget.

As you stare at it, you hear footsteps. Abraham is approaching you. "How's it coming so far?" he asks. He glances toward your open palm. "Did you find something already?"

- To lie and tell Abraham you haven't had any luck, turn to page 27.
- To show him your find, turn to page 29.

You just want to get started panning. You shake your head. "Sorry," you say. "Thanks for the offer, but I really need to start setting up."

The man nods. "Good luck to you then," he says.

You continue to the riverbank. You find a spot in a stand of trees and set up your camp. It's not much—just a canvas tarp and some blankets. But you're not here for comfort. You're here for gold.

It's late afternoon. Many of the prospectors are packing up for the night. But you're eager to start. You take your pan and wade into the cold, shallow water. You scoop up some silt and start swirling your pan, letting the lighter material spill over the edge and the heavier pieces sink.

Nothing. Just rocks and silt. You try again and again. Nothing.

Turn the page.

Disgusted, you throw your pan down, splashing it into the water. You imagined finding gold right away. But you can see that this won't be that easy.

The sun is dipping low in the sky. In the distance, a bolt of lightning flashes. Moments later, a boom of thunder rolls over the landscape. You're the only one still in the water.

- To pack up for the night, go to the next page.
- To keep trying, turn to page 37.

You sigh. Clearly, this is going to be harder than you thought. You head back to the riverbank and throw your gear to the ground. You spend the next 20 minutes trying to start a fire, but with no success.

"Having a tough start?" a voice calls out from behind you. You turn to see Abraham—the man who greeted you when you arrived here. "Can I help?" he asks.

"Please," you reply. Abraham pulls a flint out of his pocket. He strikes it, creating a bright orange spark. Within minutes, you have a nice little fire.

The two of you talk for a few minutes. Abraham suggests that you try a spot upstream, away from the others. "There's gold here," he assures you. "We just have to find the right place."

Turn the page.

By morning, you're feeling confident. You move upstream and find a nice spot at a bend in the river. You get to work, scooping up sand and silt, searching for that magical glint of gold. And this time, you get lucky, finding a small grain of gold. It's only a fraction of an ounce, but it's a start. You work through the day, adding a few more grains and flakes along the way. You store your treasure in a small pouch, carefully dropping in each precious bit of gold as you find it.

Late that afternoon, Abraham calls out to you from the banks. "Any luck?" he asks. You quickly glance down to your hand, which holds yet another small grain of gold.

- To tell Abraham you haven't had any luck, turn to page 27.
- To show off what you've found, turn to page 29.

This isn't what you'd imagined. There are dozens of people panning in this stream. How can you hope to get rich? "Let's go on," you say. Kalapine nods and leads the way.

Turn the page.

The ground gets more and more rugged. Your legs ache, and your clothes are drenched in sweat. But finally, just as the sun is setting, you arrive at another small stream, deep in the wilderness. It's late, so Kalapine camps the night with you. You build a small fire and sleep under the stars. When you wake up in the morning, she is already gone. You're disappointed you didn't get to say goodbye.

You scan the creek ahead. It's small—no more than waist deep. But it's fast-moving, and its sandy bottom is ideal for panning.

As you stand on the banks of the stream, you hear a deep growl. Slowly, you turn around. A large grizzly bear emerges out of the trees. It was probably headed to the river to look for fish. The huge animal towers over you. It looks ready to charge.

- To run away, turn to page 39.
- To shout at the bear, turn to page 41.

You quickly close your fist and shake your head. "Nothing yet," you say, your voice cracking. You've always been a terrible liar. "Thanks for asking."

Abraham shrugs, wishes you luck, and moves along. You're working a bit upstream from most of the others. It's quiet, aside from the sound of water running over the shallow, sandy bank.

Your luck is just beginning. For the rest of the day, you keep it up. Slowly, your pouch fills with flakes and grains of brilliant gold. It's got to be five ounces at least—and this is your first day!

You run the numbers through your mind. At $20 per ounce, you've found at least $100 in gold already. It's a massive sum—months and months of work in almost any other job.

Turn the page.

You keep at it for the next few days. You find less and less each day, but you're still doing very well. In the evening, you spend time with Abraham and the other prospectors. You try not to hint at how well you've done. When they ask how much you've found, you shrug and say, "Oh, maybe half an ounce so far."

After about a week, Abraham tells you he's headed back to a nearby town to sell his gold. "Want to join me?" he asks. "The road is safer with a friend."

You're not finding as much now as when you started. And Abraham is right about safety in numbers. But are you ready to pack up your things already?

- To go with Abraham, turn to page 31.
- To keep panning, turn to page 34.

You're so excited that you can't help but tell Abraham. "Look at that!" he says. "Not exactly a big find, but it's a great start."

Abraham walks off, whistling a tune. You get back to work. Over the next 30 minutes, you find several more small nuggets and flakes of gold, which you carefully store in a pouch. Everything is going so well. You've found a fantastic spot.

But word of your find spreads. Soon, Abraham is panning several yards upstream. More prospectors follow. In no time, more than a dozen people are panning the spot you found.

You made a mistake. You should have kept your strike quiet. Now other people are finding huge nuggets of gold—nuggets that could have been yours. The gold gets harder and harder to find. After a few days, people abandon this site altogether.

Turn the page.

Your pouch isn't empty. You've found close to an ounce of gold. But it could have been so much more. Who knows if you'll ever get that lucky again?

THE END

To follow another path, turn to page 9.
To learn more about the Gold Rush, turn to page 101.

After a moment's thought, you nod your head. "That's a good idea," you tell Abraham. The two of you pack your things and say some goodbyes. Your pouch of gold is heavy in your pocket. It thumps against your thigh every time you take a step. You can't help but grin.

About halfway to town, the two of you come over a hill. Standing before you are three men on horses.

"Well, well, what have we here?" says one of them. He grins a half-toothless smile. "Looks like prospectors!"

The other two men stare at you. They move their horses to each side of the path, trying to cut you off. With a chill, you realize they plan to rob you.

Turn the page.

But then Abraham reaches for his belt and pulls out a revolver. He fires a warning shot into the air. The crack of the gunshot echoes off the hilly landscape. "Back off!" he orders.

To your surprise—and relief—the bandits back away. You and Abraham pass and quickly put as much distance as you can between yourselves and the thieves.

"Can't be too careful," Abraham tells you. "Now, let's go cash in. I aim to spend some of my earnings on a nice, warm bath tonight."

You chuckle. "Now that sounds like a good plan," you agree. You'll enjoy your success tonight. But tomorrow, you'll head back out again. There's more gold out there, and you plan to find as much of it as you can.

THE END

To follow another path, turn to page 9.
To learn more about the Gold Rush, turn to page 101.

You shake your head. "Sorry, Abraham. It feels like I just got here. I want to find a lot more before I head back to town."

Abraham nods. "Okay, have it your way. But be careful out here."

With that, Abraham is gone. You spend two more weeks panning. Soon, your pouch is completely full of gold. You're carrying a small fortune in your pocket, and it makes you nervous. It's time to sell.

But as you pack your things, two shadows fall over you. You turn to see a pair of men standing over you. One wears a wide-brimmed hat. You recognize him—Zeke. He's been panning just downstream from you the past few days.

"Couldn't help but notice you doing well out here," he says.

The other man is a stranger. He's huge, with broad shoulders and a thick neck. A gun holster hangs from his belt. "Now hand over the gold, and you can keep your life."

For a moment, you consider running, shouting for help, or fighting. But you quickly realize those options are hopeless. The big man's hand rests on the revolver hanging at his side.

Turn the page.

Your shoulders slump as you reach into your pocket and pull out your pouch of gold. You toss it to Zeke, noticing the heavy thump as it hits the palm of his hand.

You feel numb watching the men leave with your fortune. But you suppose it could have been worse. Maybe you're lucky just to be alive.

In any case, you're not sure that panning is the life for you. Weeks of an aching back, slumped over the water, and it was all for nothing? No, thank you. Maybe you'll head back to town and find a nice job as a store clerk. That's sure to be a much less dangerous way to earn a living.

THE END

To follow another path, turn to page 9.
To learn more about the Gold Rush, turn to page 101.

You shake your head. "This spot isn't working," you mutter. You wade deeper, to a spot where the water rises up to your waist.

You reach down and scoop up a panful of sand and silt. It's so deep here that you have to dip your whole body into the chilly stream. But everyone pans the shallows. Maybe the deeper part of the stream is untapped.

You bring up your pan and start to swirl. What you find takes your breath away. "Gold," you whisper. Sure enough, there in the bottom of your pan lie several tiny nuggets of the precious metal.

You shiver. You'd swear that you were only up to your waist in water. But now, it's up to your chest. Did you stray deeper by accident?

Turn the page.

You reach down again, scooping up more sand. As you swirl, the current laps against your shoulders. Too late, you realize the danger—a thunderstorm. That means rain. The stream is rising rapidly, and you're in the middle of it.

The current grows stronger by the second. Your try to fight your way to shore, clutching your gold in one hand. But it's hopeless. The rush of water carries you downstream. You fight to stay afloat, never letting go of your precious gold.

But you fail. The currents pull you under. You hold on as long as you can. But you're not a strong swimmer. The cold waters rush over you. Your hand clutches the small, precious nuggets even to your last breath.

THE END

To follow another path, turn to page 9.
To learn more about the Gold Rush, turn to page 101.

Every instinct tells you to run. So that's what you do. You turn and sprint along the bank of the river.

Grizzlies are predators. They have instincts too. Their instinct is to chase. The moment you run, you look like prey to the bear. And that's a bad thing. The bear charges.

Turn the page.

It's no contest. You can't outrun a bear. The huge animal closes the distance to you in seconds. With a swat of its massive paw, it knocks you to the ground.

You try to get away, but it's hopeless. You came out here to look for gold. Sadly, you never even got the chance.

THE END

To follow another path, turn to page 9.
To learn more about the Gold Rush, turn to page 101.

If you run, you're pretty sure he'll catch you. What else can you do?

"Hey bear!" you shout at the top of your voice. You wave your arms and even take a few steps forward toward the big animal.

The bear had looked like it was about to charge. But your behavior changed its mind. By making yourself look big and loud, you have convinced it that you are a threat—not prey. After a few moments, the animal turns and lumbers back into the forest.

It's a reminder that every day—every moment—is dangerous out here. But the rewards are tremendous. Kalapine was right about this spot. The stream is rich with gold. There's no one else here, so that means that it's all yours.

Turn the page.

Panning is a slow process. You search one pan at a time, filling it with silt and sand and swirling it to separate the light and heavy particles. But as the days and weeks pass, you add more and more flakes of precious gold to your collection.

You're not going to get rich this way. But you'll be able to sell this gold for a good price. Maybe it will be enough to buy some land—to start a farm of your own. Many who have come here have failed to find anything. You're grateful to be one of the success stories.

THE END

To follow another path, turn to page 9.
To learn more about the Gold Rush, turn to page 101.

CHAPTER 3

DIGGING DEEP

Dust kicks up behind your boots as you storm down a dirt road headed out of a small gold-rush town. Furious, you kick at a rock and let out a shout.

That's when you hear footsteps coming up behind you. You brace yourself. As a Black freedman in 1850, you know that you won't be welcome everywhere. You just found that out firsthand. You asked the banker in the town's small bank to partner with you in a gold mining operation. He laughed in your face.

Turn the page.

A miner using a machine called a rocker box

The footsteps you hear belong to a young woman. She holds her dainty hat as she runs to you. "Hey mister," she calls out. You realize that she can't be more than 25 years old.

"Yes ma'am," you reply.

"I overheard you in the bank. I heard that man . . . my uncle . . . laugh at you. I just wanted to say I'm sorry."

You nod and smile. Racism is widespread out here. But there are still kind people.

"You told my uncle you needed $100 to get started. I have it." She goes on to explain that her husband, a gold miner, recently passed away. He left her quite a bit of money, and she's looking for an investment.

Turn the page.

You take a step back. You did not expect this. "Now understand, I offered your uncle 20 percent of everything I make. That could amount to nothing, or a whole lot, depending on my luck. Are you prepared for that kind of risk?"

The girl nods. "I'm Anna, by the way."

You introduce yourself and shake Anna's hand. Her grip is stronger than you expected.

With that, the deal is struck. You use Anna's investment to buy the pickaxes, drills, and other equipment you need to start a basic mine. You know it's a long shot that you'll strike it rich. But your whole life has been a long shot. Born an enslaved person, your enslaver took a liking to you and eventually freed you. You've spent the last year trying to earn enough money to free your brother and sister, who are still enslaved out east.

When you heard about the California Gold Rush, you had to come. Before today, you didn't have a dollar to your name and little chance to make one. Now at least you have a chance.

Prospectors have set up small mines in the hills around the American River. The ground is largely loose gravel. Gold mining is mainly a matter of hard work. But that's the only kind of work you've known.

You find a spot that looks untouched. The rolling hills are beautiful. You know that mining destroys a lot of that beauty. But you can't think about that. You need to get started.

For two days, you dig. You swing the heavy pickaxes to break up the rock. Then you use a box called a rocker to separate the rock, dust, and—hopefully—gold. But after two days of backbreaking work, you haven't found so much as a glittering flake.

Turn the page.

On the third day, a young man passes by with a donkey. The animal is loaded with packs. "Looks like you're having trouble," the man calls out. "Why not take a shortcut?" He reaches into a pack and pulls out a few red sticks. "Dynamite will speed up the process. Want to buy some?"

You have no experience with dynamite and very little money left. Is it worth a shot?

- To decline and get back to work, go to the next page.
- To buy the dynamite, turn to page 53.

You don't know a thing about dynamite. You're more likely to blow yourself up than you are to find gold with it. "No thanks," you call back. The man tips his cap to you and rides on.

You get back to work. Late on your third day, you make your strike. You dump yet another load of broken rock into your rocker box and start to sift through the contents. Then something glints in the evening sun. With a gasp, you reach into the box and pull out a gold nugget. A quick check with your teeth tells you it's the real thing—it's softer than regular rock.

And that's just the start. You chip away at that spot, deeper and deeper. Most of the nuggets are little, but you find a few larger ones too. There's a small fortune here—probably 35 ounces or more.

Turn the page.

You head back into town. Anna is at the bank with her uncle. You call out to her and show her what you've found. You're both thrilled. The banker gives you $600 for all of it, and you hand Anna her $120 cut.

"Wow, that was fast," she says. "I can't wait to see how much we make next time!"

You hesitate. You've got almost $500. That's more money than you've ever had. It might be enough to free your family. Should you try to earn a little more, to be sure it's enough? Or should you call it quits now and head east?

- To return to your mine, turn to page 55.
- To quit and head east, turn to page 65.

You sigh. So far, you've had no luck at all. A few sticks of dynamite could be worth days of work. Maybe it's worth a shot.

The man grins as you hand over your money. He plops a small bunch of dynamite in your hand and rides off, whistling a tune.

You don't know much about dynamite. But how complicated could it be? You spend some time digging a deep hole into the face of the hill. Then you set your dynamite, strike a match, and light the fuse.

You turn and run, taking shelter behind a tree. You hold your breath for 10 seconds, but nothing happens.

You're not sure what to do. Did you not give it enough time? Or did you get swindled?

Turn the page.

"I bet that's not dynamite at all!" you hiss, furious that the man swindled you. You're so frustrated, you don't know what to do. Should you just go throw out the "dynamite" and get back to work? Or should you give it more time and see what happens?

- To go back to work, turn to page 62.
- To wait a few moments, turn to page 63.

You have a feeling there's more gold to be found in your spot. Why stop now? You've made more money in just a few weeks than you've ever seen in your life. You can't stop now. You head back to your mine.

A small mine

Turn the page.

Most prospectors never find a fraction of what you've found already. You know that you've been lucky. But you've also worked hard. For the next month, you keep chipping away. You work 12-hour days. Your arms and back ache from the work. But you keep going until you've gotten all that you can from your mine.

With almost $3,000 in your pocket—after giving Anna her cut of the profits—you're becoming rich by the standards of the day. You head into Sacramento, the nearest big city, and hire a lawyer to buy your family's freedom. You'll let him work out the details while you go back to mining. You've become obsessed with gold. You don't even sell all of it anymore. You keep the most beautiful nuggets for yourself. You polish them, feel them, even sleep with them under your pillow.

With your mine dried up, it's time for your next move. Should you invest in better equipment to expand your mine? Or would it be faster just to move to a nearby hill and start digging a fresh one again?

- To use your money for better equipment, turn to page 58.
- To move to a new spot with your current gear, turn to page 67.

There's only so much you can do by hand. It's time to go big. After talking to Anna, you agree to invest your earnings in state-of-the-art equipment. The mechanical gear is expensive, but it tears through rock at speeds you could never match by hand.

You build your business, buying up land and hiring crews to run your machinery. The money rolls in, and the business grows. It's hard at times. Racism still runs deep, and some people refuse to do business with a Black man. Luckily, Anna steps in. She helps you run the business and makes deals to grow it.

After a few years, it becomes harder and harder to find gold. The business is still profitable. But the big strikes are fewer and farther between.

"We should look into silver mining," Anna suggests one day. "It's not as precious as gold. But there's a real market. Maybe it's the future for us."

"Hmm," you reply. "I'm not sure. We're a gold mining company. Why change a successful business model?

Anna shrugs. "Times change. We have to be flexible. But it's your choice."

- To tell her no, turn to page 60.
- To agree to the idea, turn to page 68.

You shake your head. "We built this business on mining gold. And look where it's taken us! No, we have to keep going, even through the tough times."

So that's what you do. You have a few lean years. The Gold Rush ends. What gold exists out here is becoming harder and harder to find. But you have the equipment that most people don't. So you keep going.

A few profitable mines turn your luck around. By 1860, your company is one of the biggest mining companies in California. One day, your work takes you near the spot where you first started mining. You remember how beautiful the land was. Now it's stripped bare. The ground is like a scar on the landscape. A wave of sadness washes over you.

You've got more money than you'll ever need.

Do you want to keep abusing the land this way?

A mine scarring the landscape

- To stop mining and work to restore the land, turn to page 70.

- To keep building mines, turn to page 72.

You stomp back to the hillside seething with anger. You reach into the hole to pull out the worthless dynamite. But as you do, you notice a sound. It's the crackling of the dynamite's fuse. With a rush of dread, you realize that you didn't wait long enough. The fuse hadn't yet reached the explosive!

You turn to run. But your luck goes from bad to worse. The blast sends rock and gravel flying through the air. The force lifts you off your feet. You land with a thud.

You took a big gamble. Unfortunately, it cost you your life.

THE END

To follow another path, turn to page 9.
To learn more about the Gold Rush, turn to page 101.

You put your head in your hands, muttering to yourself. How could you be so foolish?

What you don't realize is that the dynamite wasn't a dud. The fuse is still burning. And when it explodes, it shakes the ground and sends bits of rock screaming through the air. A few small pebbles slam into you, causing you to yelp in pain. But as the dust settles, you realize that you're not seriously hurt.

You're lucky to be alive. But that's where your luck ends. You underestimated the size of the blast. The dynamite did its job, tearing a huge hole in the hillside. Sadly, it also destroyed most of your equipment. It's worthless now.

You can't face the thought of going back to town to tell Anna about your failure. And nobody there will ever help you again, knowing how badly you messed up this chance.

Turn the page.

It's time to move on. Mining for gold was not for you. You walk west. You'll head for the coast. Maybe there's another way to earn a living out here. You may have given up on mining, but you'll never give up on your family. It's time to start over again.

THE END

To follow another path, turn to page 9.
To learn more about the Gold Rush, turn to page 101.

Anna is disappointed when you tell her you're quitting.

"Well, I guess I made a profit," she says. "But I really hoped we could be in business together for a lot longer."

You say your goodbyes and prepare for your journey. It's weeks of travel by horseback and train, but you make it back.

The journey takes up more of your money than you'd hoped. By the time you get back, you have enough left to free only your sister. The two of you head north, vowing that you'll save the rest to buy your brother's freedom as soon as you can.

Life is hard, even in the north. You eventually free your brother. Years later, you both serve the Union in the Civil War.

Turn the page.

Even during the toughest times, you think back to your brief adventure in California. Should you have stayed longer? Or did you do the right thing by leaving when you did? One thing is for sure. You'll never forget the kindness of a stranger and how Anna helped you save your family.

THE END

To follow another path, turn to page 9.
To learn more about the Gold Rush, turn to page 101.

Your system is working for you. Why change? You find a new spot and start again. At first, you find a few nuggets. But then your mine goes cold.

One day, you make a big mistake. You swing your pickaxe at a rock, just as you've done a thousand times. But you miss. The sharp point drives into your right foot.

The wound is bad. You limp into town. The local doctor can't do much to help you. You have broken bones that won't ever heal properly.

Your mining days are over. You've saved enough money to live on, but your injury leaves you unable to do manual labor. That's the only kind of work you've ever known. Your time in California was a success. But it came at a price, and you'll have to live with that the rest of your life.

THE END

To follow another path, turn to page 9.
To learn more about the Gold Rush, turn to page 101.

You owe Anna so much. She took a shot on you when nobody else would, and she was right to do it. She's been right about many of the deals that have helped grow your business too. You feel like you owe it to her to do what she wants. So you agree to switch your business to focus on silver mining.

It sounds like an easy switch. But it's not that simple. Silver mining is a whole different process.

You invest huge sums in new equipment. When your first mines fail, the business is in trouble. But you feel loyal to Anna. You pour more money into the effort, but the business is losing money fast.

Within two years, you are bankrupt. The money is gone. Once again, you are broke.

The mining life treated you well. You were able to buy your family's freedom and enjoy a wealthy lifestyle for a few years. But now, you're back to living day-to-day. Like many other miners, you learned that prospecting is a boom-or-bust business. You enjoyed the boom. Now you have to live with the bust.

THE END

To follow another path, turn to page 9.
To learn more about the Gold Rush, turn to page 101.

"What am I doing?" you mutter to yourself. The ruined landscape fills you with sadness. Your mining operation did this.

You decide that it's just not worth it anymore. You and Anna are both rich beyond your wildest dreams. You scale back your business. You stop buying new mines. You've taken enough from the land. Now it's time to give back.

Miners working at Cavaleras River

For the rest of your life, you devote yourself to restoring the environment. You push for laws that protect the land from mining. You become a force in California and national politics, pushing for change. Again, many people don't want to hear it from a Black person, but that doesn't stop you.

It's not about the money anymore. You and your family are free. Legal enslavement has come to an end by 1865. Now what matters is building a better future for everyone. And you're doing all you can to be part of the solution.

THE END

To follow another path, turn to page 9.
To learn more about the Gold Rush, turn to page 101.

You shake your head, but you tell yourself that this is just the cost of the mining business. So you keep going. Your business grows and grows. By 1870, it's one of the biggest mining operations in the country.

Your mining efforts spell disaster for the land and the people who live there—including native peoples. Some beg you to stop. But you don't listen. All that matters is finding more gold and getting more money. You—a freed slave—are a leader in industry. You stand as an example of what anyone can do with a little luck and a lot of hard work. So what if your fortune has destroyed some land and trees? You'll keep mining as much gold as you can until the day you die.

THE END

To follow another path, turn to page 9.
To learn more about the Gold Rush, turn to page 101.

CHAPTER 4

FROM GOLD RUSH TO GHOST TOWN

"Here kid, this is for your trouble."

The old man flips a quarter into your palm. You fight back a grin. It's an outrageous tip. But here in Angels Creek, money has flown fast and loose. It's 1852, and the Gold Rush has been going on for a few years. You've been serving as a bellhop at the local saloon. You help visitors with their bags and give them the inside information on the town. Basically, you try to make yourself useful in any way that you can.

Turn the page.

Angels Creek is in the heart of gold country. Many of the people who pass through have made a fortune mining gold. You've lived in this part of California all your life, working a small farm with your parents. But all that changed in 1848, when gold was discovered in the American River. Suddenly, California went from an overlooked U.S. territory to a booming economy. Countless towns like Angels Creek have sprung up almost overnight. It's your home—for now. But you know that this boom can't last forever. You're just happy to ride it as long as you can.

Of course, like most young people here, you tried your hand at panning for gold. You failed at that, but that doesn't mean you can't make some money off the Gold Rush in northern California. Your sister has made hundreds of dollars selling home-cooked food to miners. You're always on the lookout for opportunities to cash in too.

An early settlement in California

"Thank you, sir," you say. You close your fist around the quarter, squeezing it tight.

Turn the page.

The old man, who introduces himself as Hank, takes off his hat and sits down on the wooden chair in the small room.

"You seem like a capable young person," he says. "Would you have any interest in taking on a job for me?"

You raise an eyebrow. Of course, you're always looking for a way to earn some money.

"I run a bank based out of Sacramento. Some of our gold shipments have been robbed recently. I'm looking for guards who can make sure that the gold arrives safely. Are you interested?"

You scratch your chin. "It sounds dangerous," you say.

Hank smiles. "You will be well paid," he says. "I'll make it worth your while. What do you say, son?"

It might be a good opportunity. Crime is a big problem out here. But then again, it could be dangerous. Money isn't worth anything if you're dead. Hank awaits your answer.

A miner with his tools and gold

- To take the job, turn to page 80.
- To decline, turn to page 82.

You've always been the type of person to jump at an opportunity. This is no different. "You've got a deal, sir," you say, shaking Hank's hand.

The next day, you join Hank outside of town. A large man with a bushy beard stands at his side. "This is Robert," Hank says. "I hired him last week. I need the two of you to get a shipment of gold to the bank in Sacramento.

Hank leads you to three horses. Two of them are saddled. The third carries a load of saddlebags. They hang heavily to either side of the horse. "There's thousands of dollars in gold here," Hank explains. "Every bit is accounted for. I'll expect it all in Sacramento by tomorrow evening."

You and Robert head west out of town along a dirt trail. About an hour later, four men emerge from behind a stand of trees. They wear bandanas over their faces. Each man holds a revolver.

"Stop right there," the leader calls out. He's a skinny man with a long scar down the side of his face. "Just turn around and leave the gold. Nobody has to get hurt here."

Your hands are shaking. You knew this was possible. You're glad to have Robert by your side. But when you turn to him, he's smiling.

"Sorry kid," he says. "I didn't mean for you to get caught up in this. Didn't know old Hank would go and hire a second guard."

Your heart sinks. Robert is one of the bandits.

"You know," Robert continues. "You could just join us. There's plenty of gold to go around, and we can always use an extra man. What do you say? Are you up for a life of crime?

- To refuse, turn to page 84.
- To join the bandits, turn to page 86.

If you wanted danger, you'd be out there looking for gold yourself. "Thanks for the offer, sir," you say. "I'm not sure that's the job for me. Anyway, enjoy your stay."

You step outside onto the sunbaked main street of Angels Creek. Wooden buildings line the street. A few horses stand by a hitching post in front of the saloon. Down the road, are the general store and the bank.

The town is growing quiet. There was a time when main street was almost always buzzing. Two years ago, this town was bursting with activity. But the Gold Rush has slowed. Many of the prospectors have moved on.

For the next few months, you do odd jobs. You continue to work at the saloon. You help mind the general store. You even take on some mail delivery. But with each year that passes, the town seems to grow less and less busy.

You like it here. The town has become your home. Everyone knows you and trusts you. But the few visitors that come through can't stop talking about San Francisco. Unlike Angels Creek, that city is thriving.

Should you pack your things and head for new opportunities in San Francisco? Or should you stay put here, making your living in the town you've grown to love?

- To go to San Francisco, turn to page 89.
- To stay here, turn to page 91.

There's no way you're signing up for a life of crime. You throw down your weapon and slowly back away.

"Umm . . . Robert," calls out one of the bandits. "The kid knows your name and face. Do we really want to let him go?"

You don't give Robert time to think about that. With a kick, you take off at top speed.

Your horse is faster than you'd guessed. You quickly put distance between yourself and the bandits.

You're worried that they'll follow you. But a look over your shoulder shows you there is nothing to worry about. They've got their big score. You're relieved that it looks like they're content to let you go.

As you ride back toward town, your mind is racing. What will you tell Hank? And will he even believe you? He might think you stole the gold. Or that you helped Robert. Do you dare go back? You've heard people in town talk about how great San Francisco is. Maybe you should start a new life there instead.

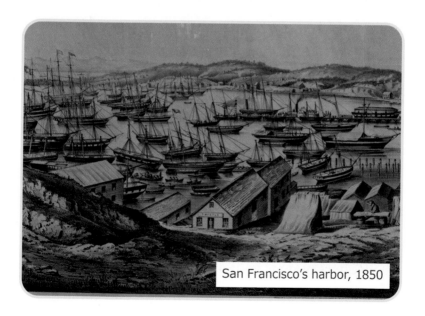

San Francisco's harbor, 1850

- To return to town, turn to page 88.
- To head west toward San Francisco, turn to page 89.

The men stare at you with their hands on their weapons. If you say no, they'll probably shoot you. You can identify Robert to the authorities.

Your voice trembles as you answer, "Okay."

With that, you become an outlaw. There are five others in the gang. Evenly split six ways, the gold in Hank's shipment is a huge amount. "But it's not enough," Robert says. "There's so much more. The Gold Rush won't last forever. We have to take every dime we can before it's gone."

A week later, you come upon two prospectors headed to town after doing some panning in a nearby stream.

Robert nudges you out onto the trail. "This is your chance," he says. "Get that gold and show us that you've got what it takes."

You step out. Robert and one other man stand behind you. You take a gulp and try to sound like a dangerous criminal.

"Well, well, what have we here?" you say. You hope the two frightened men don't hear the crack in your voice. "Looks like prospectors!"

One of the men reaches for a revolver. You're willing to steal from them. But you don't want to hurt them. You have to act fast. Do you charge at them, hoping the man is bluffing. Or do you just give up and run away?

• To charge, turn to page 97.
• To run away, turn to page 98.

Hank was counting on you, and your shipment of gold is gone. You have to go back to face the music.

At first, he looks angry when you tell him what happened. But then he lets out a big sigh and pats you on the back. "I'm sorry I put you in that situation," he says. "I didn't realize Robert was a dangerous man." You're surprised when Hank pays you in full for the job, even though you never made it to Sacramento.

A few days later, Hank heads back to Sacramento. Your time as a guard didn't last long. You get back to doing odd jobs around town. But as the months pass, there's less and less work to be found. The Gold Rush is slowly ending. Towns like Angels Creek are turning into ghost towns. You look down main street and wonder how much longer it will survive.

• Turn to page 91.

The Gold Rush has taught you to be ready to change at a moment's notice. This is one of those times. There's nothing left for you in Angels Creek. It's time to head west. In the past few years, San Francisco has boomed from a little town of about 450 people to a thriving city. You'll head there to find the next chapter in your life.

When you arrive, you can hardly believe what you see. Buildings sprawl out along the bay. Ships pack the city's harbor. Smoke rises from hundreds of buildings.

You walk the streets, taking in the sights. As you wander, you spot several HELP WANTED signs. One is for a blacksmith's apprentice. You'd work for the blacksmith while learning a valuable trade. The work would be hard, and you wouldn't make much money at first, but it could lead to a good career.

Turn the page.

Another sign is for a logging company. Demand for building supplies has soared. The company wants people to help cut down trees and turn them into lumber. The job pays well.

- To take the blacksmith job, turn to page 93.
- To become a logger, turn to page 95.

Patrick, the owner of the general store, walks by. He waves and calls out your name. "Care to mind the shop for me this afternoon?" he asks.

"Sure, no problem," you respond. It's good work, and you've become great friends with Patrick and his young family. You realize that you can't leave Angels Creek. The town and the people just mean too much to you. You'll stick it out here as long as you can.

The next few months are rough. The town's bank closes. When that happens, the few remaining prospectors in the area stop coming here altogether. Patrick keeps the store open as long as he can. But there's just not enough business for him to support his family.

By the summer of 1856, Angels Creek is a ghost town. Its wooden buildings are boarded up. Its streets are silent. You are its final resident.

Turn the page.

You shake your head as you pack your things and hit the road. It's time to find a new home. Maybe you'll head east, or south, toward Mexico. Wherever you go, you're sure to find adventure. The Gold Rush may be over, but there's always a new opportunity around the corner.

THE END

To follow another path, turn to page 9.
To learn more about the Gold Rush, turn to page 101.

You've worked one job after the next all your life, never settling down. Maybe it's time to learn a trade. You could start your own business someday. Maybe even settle down and have a family.

You sign on to work as a blacksmith's apprentice. You work in a small shop, learning from Jonathan, the resident blacksmith.

Your shop specializes in building tools, from pickaxes to shovels. You learn how to heat steel and iron and pound it into shape.

It's hard work but a fun challenge. You spend long days sweating over molten-hot fires. But with time, you get good at the job. After a few years, you open your own shop, specializing in making horseshoes.

Turn the page.

It's a good living. You become a respected member of the community. You get married and start a family of your own. Even though the Gold Rush is over, California is still growing rapidly. You're an important part of its vibrant economy. You have good reason to feel proud of yourself.

THE END

To follow another path, turn to page 9.
To learn more about the Gold Rush, turn to page 101.

A blacksmith shop

You want to make money now, and the logging job pays better. So you sign up. The company sends you north to dense forest land. You take a ship along the Pacific Coast. The forests, hills, and mountains show off the area's natural beauty.

Of course, that beauty ends as soon as you reach the logging site. The land here is stripped bare. It looks like a giant tear on the earth.

Mr. Thomas, your crew manager, comes up behind you. "I know, it's not pretty. But they're just trees, right? They'll grow back, in time."

The next day, you start logging. One team uses huge saws to cut down trees. You work with a team of horses to pull the fallen trees to a river that winds through the area. From there, you float the trees down to a sawmill, where they cut the wood into lumber. It's loaded onto ships and carried all around California.

Turn the page.

You don't mind the hard work. But destroying so much natural beauty bothers you. After a year, you've saved up a lot of money. You quit the job and hit the road again.

What's next? You don't know. All your life, you've drifted from job to job. It would be nice to settle down. But this is your life. You're on to the next adventure.

THE END

To follow another path, turn to page 9.
To learn more about the Gold Rush, turn to page 101.

You think he's bluffing. You need to show that you mean business. You charge at the two men, shouting to intimidate them. One man turns and runs away, but the one with the gun holds his ground

You doubt he'll shoot. You just have to scare him into giving up his gold. You take a few more steps, preparing to grab his gold. But you were wrong. A shot rings out, echoing across the countryside.

At first, you think he missed. But then you feel the pain in your chest. You fall to your knees. Your shirt is already wet with blood.

The world goes dark. You chose a life of crime, and now you've paid the price. Your adventure ends here.

THE END

To follow another path, turn to page 9.
To learn more about the Gold Rush, turn to page 101.

Playing the part of a bandit might sound easy. But when you're on the wrong end of a six-shooter, you're forced into second thoughts. With a yelp, you turn and run into the forest. You hurdle over dead trees and dive behind the cover of some rocks.

In the distance, you hear Robert and his fellow bandits chuckling. "Did you see him run?" one of them says. "I think he might have wet himself!"

Moments later, the gang approaches you. The sight of you hiding behind a rock sends them into fits of laughter.

"Look kid, you're no criminal," Robert says. His voice is kind, but you can tell he's all business. "We'll take your cut of the last job. Just go on your way. Go back to a life of . . . whatever it is you do."

You don't fight it, and you're surprised that none of the other men do either. Robert must be the leader of the gang. You hand over your share of the money from Hank's shipment. Alone and broke, you head out into the wilderness.

Where will you go? What will you do? You shake your head. Whatever you choose, it can't be worse than your failed attempt at a life of crime.

THE END

To follow another path, turn to page 9.
To learn more about the Gold Rush, turn to page 101.

CHAPTER 5

THE GOLD RUSH

In 1848, a man named John Sutter hired another man named James Marshall to build a sawmill along a fork of California's American River. The two men didn't know it at the time, but they were about to change history.

In January of that year, Marshall was looking at the millrace—a channel of fast-moving water that powered the mill. He noticed something unexpected. The rushing water had revealed shining flakes of metal ore. Marshall had discovered gold!

Sutter, who owned the mill, tried to keep the discovery quiet. He quickly worked to collect as much gold as he could. But his secret got out fast. Word spread through California's sparsely populated frontier and beyond.

The news sent shock waves throughout the young United States. By 1849, thousands of people were flocking to California in hopes of striking it rich.

For some, the journey was worthwhile. Over the next four years, they extracted about $2 billion in gold from the hills and rivers of northern California. That's worth more than $70 billion by today's standards. But for every success story, there were countless tales of failure. Some people died on the dangerous journey to California. Others arrived but only found failure. They gave up everything they had and came away with little or nothing.

The Gold Rush was even worse for the land and its native peoples. Lands were stripped. Rivers were blasted by ultra-strong jets of water in a technique called hydraulic mining. Native people were forced from their lands. Many died at the hands of the miners, either from disease, starvation, or violence.

Sutter's Mill

Throughout northern California, mining towns sprung up. But most of them collapsed within just a few years, leaving many people to flock to bigger cities. California's population grew. Before Marshall's discovery, the territory was sparsely populated. The Gold Rush changed that.

In 1850, California became a state. Its capital, Sacramento, sat at the foot of the Sierra Madre mountains, in the heart of gold country. Today, California's official nickname is the Golden State.

The peak of the Gold Rush lasted from 1849 to 1852. By then, most of the easy-to-find gold was gone. The days of the independent prospector were ending. Large mining companies took over, digging ever deeper to find gold located underground.

While towns such as San Francisco and Sacramento became booming cities, many more died. Ghost towns still dot the Sierra Nevada region.

The Gold Rush brought California worldwide fame, and it kept growing even after the gold was long gone. But the damage to native people and to the land also echoes into the modern day. For some, the Gold Rush was a way to make a better life for themselves. But often, that better life came at a terrible cost to others.

A California ghost town

California Gold Rush Timeline

January 24, 1848: James Marshall discovers gold in the American River near Sutter's Mill.

December 5, 1848: U.S. President James K. Polk announces in a speech that gold has been discovered in California. As spring draws near, tens of thousands of people flock west to search for gold. The California Gold Rush begins.

April 13, 1850: California's government passes the Foreign Miners' Tax. It is designed to prevent Mexican miners from profiting from the Gold Rush.

September 9, 1850: California becomes a state.

1851: California miners discover more than $75 million worth of gold that year.

1852: The Gold Rush peaks, as miners find more than $81 million worth of gold. It is the most prosperous year of the Gold Rush.

1853: Edward Matteson develops a new mining technique called hydraulic mining. The new technique causes massive damage to the landscape.

1859: Silver is discovered in the Sierra Nevada mountains. Many miners divert their attention to silver, marking an end to the California Gold Rush.

Other Paths to Explore

1. Crime was a huge problem during the Gold Rush. For some people, prospecting for gold was harder than just stealing it. How would you feel if you were robbed after a big strike? How might the robbers feel? Would they have guilt over stealing from prospectors?

2. Many native people were not prepared for the Gold Rush. Their lands were swarmed by prospectors. They suffered from diseases and violence. How would you feel as an American Indian, watching your homelands be overrun by gold-seeking outsiders? How would you try to protect your way of life?

3. Some prospectors succeeded during the Gold Rush, but most failed. They left their homes and families. They traveled across the continent, and they came up empty. What would you do in that situation? How would you respond? How might you bounce back and build a new life after such a huge failure?

Glossary

apprentice (uh-PREN-tiss)—a person who works for and learns from a skilled professional for a set amount of time

bankrupt (BANG-krupt)—lacking the money to pay off debts

blacksmith (BLAK-smith)—a person who makes and fixes things made of iron

dynamite (DY-nuh-myt)—a material that makes a powerful explosion

economy (i-KAH-nuh-mee)—the ways in which a country handles its money and resources

freedman (FREED-man)—a person who was released from enslavement

millrace (MIL-rayss)—a channel that carries swiftly moving water to a mill, giving it power

ore (OR)—rock that contains metals or other valuable minerals

prospector (PROSS-pek-tuhr)—a person who looks for valuable minerals, especially silver and gold

revolver (rih-VOL-vur)—a type of handgun that usually has five to eight cartridges in a cylinder

sawmill (SAW-mil)—a factory that cuts logs into lumber

Selected Bibliography

Boessenecker, John. *Gold Dust and Gunsmoke: Tales of Gold Rush Outlaws, Gunfighters, Lawmen, and Vigilantes.* New York: John Wiley, 1999.

Brands, H. W. *The Age of Gold: The California Gold Rush and the New American Dream.* New York: Doubleday, 2002.

Rau, Margaret. *The Wells Fargo Book of the Gold Rush.* New York: Atheneum, 2001.

The California Gold Rush
history.com/topics/westward-expansion/gold-rush-of-1849

The Gold Rush
pbs.org/wgbh/americanexperience/features/goldrush-california/

Read More

Butler-Ngugi, Anitra. *The Real History of the Gold Rush*. Minneapolis: Lerner Publications, 2023.

Harris, Beatrice. *The California Gold Rush*. New York: Gareth Stevens Publishing, 2022.

Kim, Carol. *Sutter's Mill and the California Gold Rush: Separating Fact from Fiction*. North Mankato, MN: Capstone Press, 2023.

Internet Sites

Ducksters: California Gold Rush
ducksters.com/history/westward_expansion/california_gold_rush.php

History for Kids: California Gold Rush
historyforkids.org/california-gold-rush/

Oakland Museum of California: Gold Rush!
explore.museumca.org/goldrush/

JOIN OTHER HISTORICAL ADVENTURES WITH MORE YOU CHOOSE SEEKING HISTORY!

YOU CHOOSE

COMING TO AMERICA
THROUGH THE ANGEL ISLAND IMMIGRATION STATION

25 CHOICES
11 ENDINGS

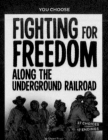

YOU CHOOSE

FIGHTING FOR FREEDOM
ALONG THE UNDERGROUND RAILROAD

37 CHOICES
17 ENDINGS

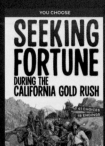

YOU CHOOSE

SEEKING FORTUNE
DURING THE CALIFORNIA GOLD RUSH

41 CHOICES
18 ENDINGS

YOU CHOOSE

TAKING A STAND
DURING THE WAR OF 1812

39 CHOICES
20 ENDINGS

About the Author

Matt Doeden is a freelance author and editor from Minnesota. He's written numerous children's books on sports, music, current events, the military, extreme survival, and much more. Doeden began his career as a sports writer before turning to publishing. He lives in Minnesota with his wife and two children.